Summary

T0366782

Historic England's Introductions to Heritage Assets (IHAs) are accessible, authoritative, illustrated summaries of what we know about a specific type of archaeological site, building, landscape or marine asset. Typically they deal with subjects which lack such a summary. This can either be where the literature is dauntingly voluminous, or alternatively where little has been written. Most often it is the latter, and many IHAs bring understanding of site or building types which are neglected or little understood. Many of these are what might be thought of as 'new heritage', that is they date from after the Second World War.

Jewish burial grounds existed in medieval England, but they were lost after the expulsion of Jews by Edward I (1290). Following a gap of over three hundred and fifty years, Jewish immigrants were allowed to settle in England. Burial space was a top priority for the newly established communities, considered more essential than a synagogue. Burial grounds therefore frequently provide the earliest physical evidence for the presence of a Jewish population.

Approximately 120 Jewish burial grounds in England date from before 1938. They are widely distributed in towns and cities where Jewish populations exist, or once existed. They have their own distinctive character and specific features which meet the religious requirements of Judaism, while also reflecting cultural traditions from their congregation's country of origin. Demographic change, decay, vandalism and pressure to free land for development mean that many Jewish burial grounds, particularly those which have long closed for new burials, face an uncertain future today.

Front cover:
Late-19th century monument styled on a Classical temple, marking H Samuel family graves (United Synagogue Cemetery, Willesden)

This document has been prepared by Nicky Smith and edited by Mark Bowden. It is one of a series of Introductions to Heritage Assets (IHAs) covering archaeological features.
This edition was published by Historic England in December 2019.
All images © Historic England unless otherwise stated.

Please refer to this document as:
Historic England 2019 Anglo-Jewish Burial Grounds: The Post Resettlement Period Swindon. Historic England.

https://historicengland.org.uk/listing/selection-criteria/scheduling-selection/ihas-archaeology/

Contents

1 Introduction

A Jewish burial ground, known variously in Hebrew as a *Bet Kevarot* (House of Graves), *Bet Hayim* (House of Life) or *Bet Olam* (House of Eternity), is a consecrated place which is sacred forever to the Jewish community. Its primary purpose is to house the bodily remains of deceased Jews. While notions of a soul and afterlife are less distinct in Judaism than in some other religions, burial grounds are considered to be occupied by the deceased and, even when closed for new interments , they are not seen as 'disused' in any sense. According to ancient Jewish tradition, the deceased await the Messianic age when Jews will be gathered from across the Earth, the bodies of the dead will be reunited with their souls and returned to Israel.

Treatment of Jewish dead is entrusted to burial societies known as the *Chevrah kadisha*. The body is washed with clear water and wrapped with a simple cloth, shroud or robe of white linen. A man may also be wrapped in his prayer shawl. The coffin is usually a plain wooden box without polished handles or other adornment in order to ensure equality in death and help the deceased to return to the dust. Since the deceased are defenceless their bodies should not be left alone, but should be watched over constantly until the funeral. Out of respect, Jewish customs avoid the use of cemeteries for activities that the dead can no longer take part in, including recreation, eating, drinking or listening to music. It is also disrespectful to step on a grave or sit on a gravestone.

2 History

2.1 Early resettlement (1656-1815)

Oliver Cromwell's decision to allow Jews to return to England after 1656 was partially motivated by his aim to re-establish London as a major trading centre and was influenced by Rabbi Menassah ben Israel of Amsterdam. The first Jewish immigrants to arrive included prosperous *Sephardi* merchants (Hebrew *Sepharad* 'Spain') who came via Holland and Portugal. They were soon joined by *Ashkenazim* (Hebrew *Ashkenaz* 'Germany') from Holland and Germany. Both groups settled and worked in the East End of London where they opened their first synagogue in Creechurch Street (1657). By 1700 the small community had grown to approximately 600 people, mainly merchants, but also contractors and dealers in bullion and diamonds and a few physicians.

The 18th century and the beginning of the 19th century saw the Anglo-Jewish population increase further. Three major synagogues were founded in London: the Sephardi Bevis Marks (1701), the Ashkenazi Hambro (1725) and New Synagogue (1761). At the same time, small communities were established in other areas of England, primarily in coastal ports and towns offering commercial opportunities.

2.2 Consolidation and emancipation (1816-1857)

The end of the Napoleonic Wars in 1815 heralded the decline of the early Jewish port communities and there was little new immigration in the first half of the 19th century. The Anglo-Jewish population was established, well-educated and had adapted to British society. A number of Jewish families in London, such as the Rothschilds and Montefiores, gained considerable economic and political power. 1842 saw the advent of Reform Judaism in England, with the foundation of the West London Synagogue of British Jews, whose services were conducted in English. The Jews Relief Act of 1858 granted Jews full political rights and in the same year Lionel de Rothschild became the first Jewish Member of Parliament.

2.3 Immigration (1858-1914)

Jewish immigration resumed in the mid-19th century and Britain's Jewish population grew steadily from 36,000 in 1858 to 60,000 in 1881, predominantly due to the arrival of Jews from Eastern Europe. The pace of immigration accelerated rapidly after 1881 following a series of pogroms and restrictions placed on Jews in the Ukraine and southern Russia.

By 1914, the Jewish population had almost tripled following the arrival of *c*150,000 new immigrants. In contrast with the earlier settlers, the majority were poor, uneducated and strictly religious. Most lived and worked in the slums of London's East End or settled in northern industrial towns, such as Manchester, Leeds and Liverpool, where large Jewish communities grew up. They formed their own *hebra* or *chevra* (benevolent societies to which a small synagogue was often attached).

The poverty of the new immigrants and their high numbers, placed a heavy burden on existing congregations. Combined with their foreign outlook and customs, this created tension with the established community. New branches of Judaism were introduced including strictly orthodox Hasidic Judaism, followers of which founded the Adath Yisroel congregation (1911) and the Union of Orthodox Hebrew Congregations (1926). At the other end of the religious spectrum, the Jewish Religious Union, founded in 1902, opened England's first Liberal Jewish synagogue in 1911.

2.4 The War years and later

The First World War ended almost a century of escalating Eastern European Jewish migration to Britain. In the inter-War period, a smaller number of Jewish refugees from Germany and Austria arrived, strengthening progressive Judaism.

During the Second World War, London's East End was severely damaged by German bombing, resulting in the movement of Jews to other parts of London. The United Kingdom's Jewish population reached a peak of *c*420,000 in the 1950s, following which it has steadily declined until the most recent Census (2012). This recorded a small increase to *c*284,000 with Jews forming 0.5% of the United Kingdom's total population.

3 Chronology and Development

Despite the high degree of respect accorded to the deceased, a fundamental belief in the impurity of the dead underpins many of the customs relating to death and burial defined in *halakhah* (Jewish religious law). For this reason Jewish burial grounds, like Roman cemeteries, were traditionally built beyond town walls and are very rarely situated next to a synagogue. The deceased must be buried as soon as possible after death to protect the living. The *Cohanim* (hereditary priests) must take particular care to avoid defilement through contact with the dead. Visitors should also ritually cleanse their hands on leaving a cemetery, for which basins with jugs are often provided at cemetery gates.

Marking a grave, while common today, is not essential according to Jewish relegious law and is not universal practice. Upright headstones (*matzevot*) of the Ashkenazi tradition are most commonly found in Anglo-Jewish cemeteries, reflecting the Central and Eastern European origins of the vast majority of Britain's Jewish population. Sephardi burial grounds have graves marked by false sarcophagi. Tombs of notable scholars and rabbis may be covered with more elaborate structures. Whatever their form, modest and understated tombstones are encouraged, in keeping with the Jewish belief that all should be equal in death. Ornamental planting and laying of floral tributes is not Jewish practice and figurative sculpture is not permitted because of a fear that it may lead to idolatry. In Liberal and Reform cemeteries such restrictions are sometimes less prescriptive.

Figure 1:
Sephardi tombs with Ashkenazi headstones in the background, Urmston Jewish Cemetery, Manchester.

The vast majority of Jewish cemeteries are plain and austere, with serried ranks of graves in gravel-covered plots. The arrangement of graves is generally chronological or by family grouping with later burials inserted next to family members. Segregation of male and female burials occurs until end of the 19th century in some Orthodox cemeteries. Infants are usually buried in separate areas, often in unmarked graves. While it is often said that Jewish burials face towards Jerusalem, in practice their alignment varies considerably and is more commonly towards the cemetery entrance. Headstones usually face towards the body, but a few have their inscriptions facing away, so visitors do not stand on the grave to read them. For the same reason, and to protect the Cohanim, the boundaries of individual graves are usually carefully delimited by kerbs.

Jewish funerals are not held in synagogues. They may be conducted at the graveside, but normally take place in the *Ohel* (Hebrew 'tent'), a special prayer hall situated in the cemetery. As well as an Ohel, a Jewish burial ground may contain a *Bet Taharah* (house of purification) where bodies are ritually washed and prepared for burial. There may also be a separate watch house or caretaker's lodge. In larger cemeteries founded by wealthy congregations, particularly in London, these buildings are often combined into elaborate complexes designed by leading architects.

Funerary buildings are commonly situated at the cemetery entrance separating the street frontage from the burial area and entry to the cemetery is often through the buildings. The Ohel invariably consists of a main hall, sometimes supplemented by a small extension with washing facilities. Wide double doors usually open onto a turning circle for hearses and carriages, while an opposing set of double doors leads into the burial area. Stained glass windows and tiled floors, frequently incorporating Star of David motifs, are common features. Furnishing is always basic, consisting of benches around side walls, or re-used church pews, memorial plaques and a lectern. Charitable donations are encouraged at funerals, so charity boxes are often built into the walls.

Buildings do not necessarily date from the period of a cemetery's construction. Some were later additions to cemeteries without buildings and older buildings were commonly renewed. The architects of most are unknown and their eclectic styles draw influences from a variety of traditions, including Byzantine, Classical and Gothic, reflecting the cultural diversity of the Anglo-Jewish community and prevailing fashions at the time of their construction. Unusual designs include several late-19th and early 20th-century octagonal Ohalim and a late-19th century Ohel resembling an engine shed at Manchester's Reform Jewish cemetery.

Figure 2:
Ohel at Manchester
Reform Cemetery, probably
built between the 1860s
and 1880s.

3.1 17th- and 18th-century burial grounds

England's earliest Jewish burial grounds were founded in London's East End soon after the re-admission of Jews in 1656. The oldest, named 'the Velho', was opened here by the first Sephardi settlers in 1657. In 1696 the Ashkenazim opened a burial ground close by, in Alderney Road, and others were soon established forming a cluster of five early Jewish burial grounds along the Mile End Road. The first Jewish burial grounds in the English provinces opened in ports along the south and east coasts in the following century. They are widely distributed from Penzance in the west to Canterbury in the east and Sunderland in the north. Originally placed away from populated centres, after several hundred years of town expansion almost all are now situated in densely urbanised areas.

They typically consist of small sub-rectangular plots some as small as 10m x 20m, their size reflecting the small Jewish population at the time of their establishment. Most are securely enclosed and concealed behind high boundary walls. Their layout is simple and functional, usually consisting of a single straight central path through a burial area with straight rows of graves. Headstones and tombs are plain in form and bear inscriptions which are wholly or predominantly in Hebrew. Some include traditional Jewish funerary symbols. The 'Cohen hands' symbol, depicting a pair of hands raised in priestly blessing, indicates that the deceased was a member of the Cohanim. A pouring pitcher, is used on the gravestone of a Levite (hereditary assistant to the Cohanim in religious services). Candelabra appear on women's gravestones, depicting the woman's role in lighting candles at home on the Sabbath. Felled tree motifs are also used regularly, indicating that the deceased's life was cut short. Some of the best examples of early Hebrew inscriptions combined with finely carved traditional Jewish symbols can be seen at Fawcett Road burial ground, Southsea.

Figure 3:
18th-century headstones in Fawcett Road Cemetery, Southsea.

3.2 Burial grounds in the early nineteenth-century

As the Jewish population increased these small burial grounds struggled to accommodate growing numbers of burials. Paths were turned into extra burial space and, despite a religious stipulation that interments should be at least six hand breadths apart, graves were packed together tightly. Where possible, burial grounds were extended, but this was not an option for those hemmed in by development. The solution to the problem at the Great, New and Hambro' Synagogues' shared burial ground in Brady Street, London, was to pile earth over existing graves to accommodate further layers of burials, a practice common in Eastern and central Europe, but rare in Anglo-Jewish cemeteries.

Figure 4:
Multiple headstones marking layered burials at Brady Street Cemetery, London.

During the 19th century the class distinction prevalent in English society began to creep into the layout of Jewish burial grounds. Separation was sometimes maintained between the burial areas of synagogue seat holders and benefactors and those of synagogue attendees who did not pay for a seat. At Brady Street the most prestigious part of the burial ground was the Great Synagogue's 'privileged members' section, added in c1810 for wealthy and influential members of the inner circle who oversaw and financed the synagogue and the burial ground. At the other end of the social scale, less affluent worshippers from the Great and Hambro' synagogues were buried in the layered area, which became known as the 'strangers' ground'.

3.3 Victorian cemeteries

Towards the end of the Georgian era, the overcrowded and insanitary state of England's urban burial grounds reached a critical point. 'Miasmas' from rotting corpses were identified as a major cause of disease. In the 1850s, a series of Burial Acts forced the closure of many urban graveyards, including several of the earliest Anglo-Jewish burial grounds in London and East Anglia. A new model for burial provision was pioneered by joint-stock companies, who opened a series of grand and picturesque suburban cemeteries in the 1830s and 1840s. The unusually elaborate Greek revival style entrance to Liverpool's Deane Road Jewish cemetery (1836) reflects these new styles in cemetery design.

Figure 5:
Neo-classical frontage to Deane Road Jewish cemetery, Liverpool. Photographed in 2002, prior to restoration.

In the second half of the 19th century extensive private Jewish cemeteries were established to serve cities with high Jewish populations. They were located on the outskirts of towns, where affordable land was available. Many were on green field sites, their plans reflecting the layout of the pre-existing landscape. At Ecclesfield, Sheffield, for example, the cemetery was established on an elongated strip field, while Manchester Urmston Cemetery re-used the southern remnant of a field recently bisected by the Manchester to Liverpool railway line. The majority of England's largest Jewish cemeteries date from this period including the United Synagogue's extensive cemeteries at Plashet (1888), West Ham (1856) and Willesden (1873), the joint Reform and Sephardi cemetery at Hoop Lane (1895) and the Western Synagogue and Federation cemeteries at Edmonton (1884 and 1889), all in London.

Established as functional spaces, Victorian Jewish cemeteries lack the ornamental landscaping seen in many non-Jewish contemporary cemeteries. The majority consist of open expanses of grave plots sub-divided by grids of paths, the layout of which is almost always based upon a central avenue leading through the burial area from the Ohel. The main avenue is often tree-lined, but ornamental trees and elaborate planting schemes are generally absent. Sub-divisions are rare but a few cemeteries, such as the United Synagogue and Liberal cemeteries at Willesden, contain small hedged or walled enclosures which serve as 'garden rooms' containing the graves of individual families. During this period Jewish burial grounds become more visible than previously, furnished with imposing entrance fronts such as the ornate wrought iron entrance gates and double prayer hall complex at Hoop Lane, Golders Green.

Figure 6:
One of several Rothschild family enclosures in the United Synagogue cemetery, Willesden.

Figure 7:
Rothschild Mausoleum,
West Ham Jewish
Cemetery, London.

In a further break with tradition, large and impressive monuments were adopted by wealthy and successful Jews. They included fashionable forms common in contemporary Christian cemeteries and a number of finely crafted bespoke tombs. Jewish families who were patrons of the arts and moved in artistic and literary circles were able to enlist the services of leading designers. They included Max Eberstadt (d1891), whose tomb in Willesden's United Synagogue cemetery was designed by family friend Edward Burne-Jones. The neo-classical Rothschild Mausoleum (1866) in West Ham Jewish cemetery, London, was designed by Sir Matthew Digby Wyatt. Although their designer is unknown, the Rothschild family's burial enclosures and tombs in the United Synagogue's Willesden cemetery are equally fine. They lie in close proximity to an imposing 'classical temple' over the graves of the Samuel family, jewellers who went on to found H Samuel jewellery shops.

Reflecting assimilation of the established Jewish community into English society, the inscriptions contain increasing amounts of English as the 19th century progresses, invariably placed below the Hebrew text. Jewish funerary images continue to be used, particularly on the graves of more recent immigrants. At Urmston cemetery, Manchester, the graves of Polish Jews display a rich array of funerary symbols more commonly seen in Eastern Europe.

The most elaborate funerary buildings date from this period and later. They are predominantly situated in London's major Jewish cemeteries, where congregations were sufficiently large and affluent to pay for their construction. Some were designed by notable Jewish architects who also designed synagogues, such as Nathan Solomon Joseph (1834-1909), who was responsible for the buildings at Willesden and Plashet cemeteries. Henry Davis(1839-1915)and Barrow Emanuel (1842-1904) designed the prayer halls at Hoop Lane as well as the West London Synagogue, the City of London School and other public buildings.

The first Jewish cremation in England took place in 1888, just four years after cremation was legalised. Camillo Roth, a Viennese member of the London Stock Exchange, was cremated and interred in Balls Pond Road Cemetery belonging to the West London Synagogue, Britain's first Jewish Reform Congregation. While still prohibited in Orthodox Judaism, cremation is acceptable In Reform and Liberal Jewish cemeteries, where under-sized graves, columbaria and lawn areas for depositing ashes can be found.

Figure 9:
Prayer halls, Hoop Lane
Cemetery, London, erected
for the cemetery's opening
in 1896.

3.4 Jewish sections in public cemeteries

The late-19th century was the great age of cemetery construction and, in 1894, the Local Government Act passed the responsibility for general cemetery provision to newly-constituted Local Authorities. Municipal cemeteries opened, like their commercial inspirations, aimed for opulent effect through imposing gateways, chapels and planting. Jewish burial was soon accommodated, by the creation of Jewish sections. One of the earliest was laid out in Southampton, where, in 1850 the town council set aside a small area for Jewish burials in its Old Common Cemetery. Deceased Jews had previously been sent to Portsmouth for burial.

Jewish sections are almost always situated on the edge of municipal cemeteries and commonly have their own separate entrance onto the street. Some are entirely self-contained, but most can also be accessed through the main cemetery gates via other burial areas. The method and degree of separation between Jewish and non-Jewish burials varies greatly. Sometimes a low rail between adjacent rows of Jewish and non-Jewish burials suffices. In other cases Jewish sections are enclosed by tall fencing or hedging, beyond which a larger space separates Jewish from non-Jewish burials. Orthodox sections generally require more separation from non-Jewish areas than Reform areas. Individual sections frequently have their own Ohel and in some cases, such as Southampton, this is designed by the main cemetery architect in the same style as the Christian cemetery chapels.

3.5 The twentieth century and later

During the 20th century opulence and obsession with social status fell from favour and Anglo-Jewish burial grounds followed a wider trend towards plainer memorials and leaner management. While Jewish cemeteries avoided modernisation into lawn cemeteries, they were kept tidy instead with coverings of gravel and regular application of weed killer.

Jewish tombstone design is generally conservative and 19th-century styles endured well into the 20th century, alongside simple and understated memorials. More elaborate styles included a series of distinctive domed tombs, such as that marking the grave of Haym Mordecai Levi (d.1923) in Urmston Cemetery, Manchester. Particularly interesting headstones and tombs from the 1920s and 1930s are found in Willesden's Liberal Jewish cemetery, where many refugees from Nazi-controlled Europe are buried. The Baron family tomb c1920, is a striking example of early-20th century funerary art, while a tomb in the form of a cylinder carried by tortoises, designed by Sir Edwin Lutyens, marks the grave of the celebrated Spanish opera star Conchita Supervia (d.1936).

Figure 10:
The grave of Haym Mordecai Levi (d.1923, Urmston Cemetery, Manchester.

Figure 11 (top):
Baron family tomb,
Willesden Liberal Jewish
cemetery, dating from
the 1920s.

Figure 12 (left):
The grave of Conchita
Supervia (d.1936),
Willesden Liberal Jewish
cemetery, London.

Several notable and distinctive Anglo-Jewish funerary buildings were also built in the early 20th century. Bournemouth East Cemetery has an unusual Ohel (1921), perhaps inspired by Charles Chipiez's reconstruction of Solomon's Temple. The Art Deco Ohel (1931) in Ecclesfield Jewish Cemetery, Sheffield, was designed by local surveyor Wynyard Dixon and reflects the architectural style of its day, in contrast to a grand triumphal arch (1938) marking the entrance to the Federation of Synagogues' cemetery at Rainham, Essex. A formal tree-lined avenue leads from the arch to the Ohel, a building with colonnaded wings designed by Lewis Solomon and Son (1937).

Hebrew inscriptions continue to be used today, with a greater proportion of English and fewer traditional Jewish symbols. The Star of David, rarely seen on early Anglo-Jewish tombstones, became increasingly popular from the 1930s and 1940s onwards and has since been adopted widely as a public confirmation of Jewishness. In contrast to hand-carved lettering and motifs on earlier memorials, inscriptions are usually sandblasted or laser-etched. The distinction between Ashkenazi and Sephardi funerary monuments has also become blurred in recent years, as ledger tombs have been adopted by some Ashkenazi congregations to prevent toppling.

A new generation of modern Jewish cemeteries situated within, or close to, the M25 was established after the mid-20th century, making extensive burial provision for London's Jewish community. Cemeteries at Cheshunt, Hertfordshire and Edgewarebury, Greater London, serve Reform, Liberal, Masorti, Sephardi and independent congregations. Silver Street Cemetery, Cheshunt, is for strictly Orthodox congregations, while the United Synagogue has an award-winning cemetery at Bushey, in Hertfordshire.

4 Associations

Jewish sections within local authority cemeteries form part of the wider cemetery landscape within which they are situated, though they do not usually share the overall landscaping scheme. Other Jewish burial grounds generally have no direct association with their surrounding features. Chatham is the only synagogue in the country with a cemetery attached to it, while Alyth (the North-Western Reform Synagogue) was built on periphery of Hoop Lane cemetery in Golders Green. A handful of Anglo-Jewish cemeteries contain war memorials, while Holocaust memorials are also found in a few cemeteries.

5 The Future

Care of cemeteries is an essential religious and social responsibility for Jews, so current burial places are carefully tended. However, maintaining closed burial grounds and extensive plots in large cemeteries which no longer generate income from new burials, is not always feasible. Funerary monuments are highly susceptible to erosion by frost action, wind and acid rain. Their heavy stone structures frequently collapse due to subsidence or undermining by burrowing animals. Damage by natural forces is compounded by vandalism, which in turn prompts demolition of derelict and unsightly structures.

The communities who founded many Jewish burial grounds were transient and moved to more affluent areas as soon as their economic circumstances allowed. The Anglo-Jewish population has also decreased significantly since the mid-20th century, due to emigration and marriage out of the faith. These factors have resulted in 'orphaned' Jewish cemeteries which no longer have attendant congregations. The Board of Deputies of British Jews has taken a lead in securing title deeds for these and some, such as Penzance Jewish burial ground and Deane Road Jewish Cemetery in Liverpool, are cared for by non-Jewish volunteers.

Several historic Anglo-Jewish burial grounds have been lost to development. The most controversial was the older part of London's Nuevo cemetery (1733), one of England's earliest Jewish burial grounds, which was redeveloped in the 1970s. The Reform Movement's first cemetery in Balls Pond Road, Islington (1843) and the United Synagogue's cemetery in Brady Street (1861) were both saved from development in the 1990s. However, many closed burial grounds occupy prime real estate in city centres, so there are powerful financial incentives for congregations to release land for development.

6 Further Reading

The first national survey of Anglo-Jewish heritage, by Dr Sharman Kadish, led to the publication of a guidebook entitled *Jewish Heritage in England* (2006). Organised by region, it provides a gazetteer of Anglo-Jewish buildings and cemeteries, giving historical background information and a description for each. An expanded and updated edition entitled *Jewish Heritage in Britain and Ireland* was published in 2015. This publication remains an essential source of information for anyone studying Anglo-Jewish heritage. For further detail on Jewish cemeteries and funerary practice, Kadish's paper 'Jewish funerary architecture in Britain and Ireland since 1656', published in *Jewish Historical Studies* (volume 43, 2011, 59-89), provides further insights. The *Archaeology of Anglo-Jewry in England and Wales 1656-c1880* by Ken Marks (2014) examines the urban topography of Anglo-Jewry prior to mass immigration from 1881 onwards, bringing together the physical evidence and background research. It provides useful descriptions of individual sites, each of which is identified on historic Ordnance Survey maps. Additional accounts relevant to the history of individual burial grounds are contained in *The Jewish Chronicle* and Historic England has produced a series of unpublished reports on a selection of cemeteries which are available from library@historicengland. org.uk (Tel: 01793 414632).

Further information may be accessed online. In 2016 'Jewish Burial Grounds: Understanding Values' was produced by Barker Langham for Historic England, highlighting the diverse values associated with historic Jewish burial grounds https://research.historicengland.org.uk/redirect. aspx?id=7015%7CJewish%20Burial%20Grounds:%20Understanding%20Values. The Cemetery Scribes website http://www.cemeteryscribes.com/ is a fruitful source of information, containing articles on cemeteries, translations of Hebrew inscriptions and photographs of headstones. Some cemeteries are yet to be recorded but, it aims to photograph and transcribe the inscriptions on each headstone of 1928 and earlier. Also of interest is the joint website of the Jewish Genealogical Society of Great Britain (JGSGB) and JewishGen https://www.jewishgen.org/JCR-UK/ This contains informative historical accounts of communities and their cemeteries, with a helpful guide to reading Hebrew inscriptions on tombstones. The websites of many synagogues also provide details of their cemetery's history.

Contact Historic England

East of England
Brooklands
24 Brooklands Avenue
Cambridge CB2 8BU
Tel: 01223 582749
Email: eastofengland@
HistoricEngland.org.uk

Fort Cumberland
Fort Cumberland Road
Eastney
Portsmouth PO4 9LD
Tel: 023 9285 6704
Email: fort.
cumberland@
HistoricEngland.org.uk

**London and
South East**
4th Floor
Cannon Bridge House
25 Dowgate Hill
London EC4R 2YA
Tel: 020 7973 3700
Email: londonseast@
HistoricEngland.org.uk

Midlands
The Axis
10 Holliday Street
Birmingham B1 1TG
Tel: 0121 625 6888
Email: midlands@
HistoricEngland.org.uk

**North East
and Yorkshire**
Bessie Surtees House
41-44 Sandhill
Newcastle Upon
Tyne NE1 3JF
Tel: 0191 269 1255
Email: northeast@
HistoricEngland.org.uk

37 Tanner Row
York YO1 6WP
Tel: 01904 601948
Email: yorkshire@
HistoricEngland.org.uk

North West
3rd Floor,
Canada House
3 Chepstow Street
Manchester M1 5FW
Tel: 0161 242 1416
Email: northwest@
HistoricEngland.org.uk

South West
29 Queen Square
Bristol BS1 4ND
Tel: 0117 975 1308
Email: southwest@
HistoricEngland.org.uk

Swindon
The Engine House
Fire Fly Avenue
Swindon SN2 2EH
Tel: 01793 445050
Email: swindon@
HistoricEngland.org.uk

Printed and bound by CPI Group (UK) Ltd, Croydon, CR0 4YY